ANTHONY DE MELLO, S.J.

THE SONG
OF
THE BIRD

IMAGE BOOKS

Division of Doubleday & Company, Inc.
Garden City, New York

1984

Image Books edition published September 1984
by special arrangement
with Center for Spiritual Exchange

Imprimi Potest: Edwin Rasquinha S.J.
                    Praep. Prov. Bomb.
                    August 26th, 1981

Imprimatur: + C. Gomes S.J.
                    Bishop of Ahmedabad
                    September 3rd, 1981

Library of Congress Cataloging in Publication Data
De Mello, Anthony, 1931–
The Song of the Bird.
1. Spiritual life—Catholic authors. 2. Story-telling
(Christian theology) I. Title.
BX2350.2.D386   1984   248.4'82

ISBN: 0-385-19615-6
Library of Congress Catalog Card Number: 84-10105
All Rights Reserved
Printed in the United States of America

THE SONG
OF
THE BIRD

CONTENTS

This book has been written for people of every persuasion, religious and nonreligious. I cannot, however, hide from my readers the fact that I am a priest of the Catholic Church. I have wandered freely in mystical traditions that are not Christian and not religious and I have been profoundly influenced by them. It is to my Church, however, that I keep returning, for she is my spiritual home; and while I am acutely, sometimes embarrassingly, conscious of her limitations and narrowness, I also know that it is she who has formed me and made me what I am today. So it is to her that I gratefully dedicate this book.

Everyone loves stories, and you will find plenty of them in this book. Stories that are Buddhist, Christian, Zen, Hasidic, Russian, Chinese, Hindu, Sufi; stories ancient and contemporary.

And they all have a special quality: if read in a certain kind of way, they will produce spiritual growth.

HOW TO READ THEM

There are three ways:

1. Read a story once. Then move on to another story. This manner of reading will give you only entertainment.

2. Read a story twice. Reflect on it. Apply it to your life. This will give you a taste of theology. This sort of thing can be fruitfully done in a group where all members share their reflections on the story. You then have a theological circle.

3. Read the story again, after you have reflected on it. Create a silence within you and let the story reveal to you its inner depth and meaning: Something beyond words and reflections. This will give you a feel for the mystical.
Or carry the story around all day and allow its *fragrance*, its *melody* to haunt you. Let it speak to your heart, not to your brain. This too could make something of a mystic out of you. It is with this mystical end in view that most of these stories were originally told.

CAUTION

Most of the stories have a comment appended to them. The comment is meant as a sample of the kind of comment you yourself may want to make. Make your own. Don't limit yourself to the ones you find in this book. Why borrow someone else's insights?

Beware of applying the story to anyone (priest, mullah, church, neighbor) other than yourself. If you do so the story will do you damage. Every one of these stories is about *you*, no one else.

When you read the book for the first time read the stories in the order in which they are set down. The order imparts a teaching and a spirit that will be lost if the stories are read haphazardly.

GLOSSARY

Theology: The art of telling stories about the Divine. Also the art of listening to them.

Mysticism: The art of tasting and feeling in your heart the inner meaning of such stories to the point that they transform you.

EAT YOUR OWN FRUIT

A disciple once complained,
>*"You tell us stories, but you never*
>*reveal their meaning to us."*

Said the master,
>*"How would you like it if someone*
>*offered you fruit and masticated it*
>*before giving it to you?"*

No one can find *your* meaning for you.
Not even the master.

A VITAL DIFFERENCE

Uwais the Sufi was once asked,
    "What has grace brought you?"

He replied,
        "When I wake in the morning I feel
        like a man who is not sure he will
        live till evening."

Said the questioner,
        "But doesn't everyone know this?"

Said Uwais,
        "They certainly do.
        But not all of them
        feel it."

No one ever became drunk on the word *wine*.

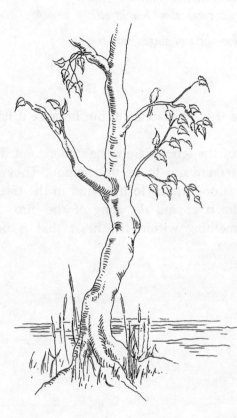

THE SONG OF THE BIRD

*The disciples were full of questions
about God.*

*Said the master, "God is the Unknown
and the Unknowable. Every statement
about him, every answer to your questions,
is a distortion of the truth."*

The disciples were bewildered. "Then
why do you speak about him at all?"

"Why does the bird sing?" said the
master.

Not because it has a statement, but because it has a song.

The words of the scholar are to be understood. The words of the master are not to be understood. They are to be listened to as one listens to the wind in the trees and the sound of the river and the song of the bird. They will awaken something within the heart that is beyond all knowledge.

THE STING

*A saint was once given the gift of
speaking the language of the ants. He
approached one, who seemed the scholarly
type, and asked, "What is the Almighty
like? Is he in any way similar to the ant?"*

*Said the scholar, "The Almighty?
Certainly not! We ants, you see, have
only one sting. But the Almighty, he
has **two!**"*

Suggested postscript:

When asked what heaven was like, the ant-scholar solemnly replied, "There we shall be just like him, having two stings each, only smaller ones."

A bitter controversy rages among religious schools of thought as to where exactly the second sting will be located in the heavenly body of the ant.

THE ELEPHANT AND THE RAT

An elephant was enjoying a leisurely dip in a jungle pool when a rat came up to the pool and insisted that the elephant get out.

"I won't," said the elephant.

"I insist you get out this minute," said the rat.

"Why?"

"I shall tell you that only after you are out of the pool."

"Then I won't get out."

But he finally lumbered out of the pool, stood in front of the rat, and said, "Now then, why did you want me to get out of the pool?"

"To check if you were wearing my swimming trunks," said the rat.

An elephant will sooner fit into the trunks of a rat than God will fit into our notions of him.

THE ROYAL PIGEON

Nasruddin became prime minister to the king.
Once, while he wandered through the palace,
he saw a royal falcon.

Now Nasruddin had never seen this kind
*of a **pigeon** before.* So he got out a
pair of scissors and trimmed the claws,
the wings, and the beak of the falcon.

"Now you look like a decent bird," he said.
"Your keeper had evidently been neglecting you."

"You're different so there's something wrong with *you!*"

MONKEY SALVATION FOR A FISH

*"What on earth are you doing?" said I
to the monkey when I saw him lift a
fish from the water and place it
on a tree.*

*"I am saving it from drowning" was the
reply.*

The sun that gives sight to the eagle blinds the owl.

SALT AND COTTON IN THE RIVER

*Nasruddin was taking a load of salt
to the market. His donkey waded through
the river and the salt dissolved. When
it reached the opposite bank the animal
ran around in circles, overjoyed that
its load had been lightened.
Nasruddin was annoyed.*

*On the next market day he packed
the panniers with cotton. The ass nearly
drowned with the increased weight
of the cotton soaked in river water.*

*"There!" said Nasruddin gleefully. "That
will teach you to think that each time
you go through water you stand to gain!"*

Two persons walked into religion.
One came alive, the other drowned.

THE SEARCH FOR THE ASS

*Everyone became alarmed when they saw
Mullah Nasruddin, astride his ass,
charging through the streets of the
village.*

*"Where are you off to, Mullah?" they
asked.*

*"I'm searching for my ass," said the
mullah as he whizzed by.*

The Zen master of Rinzai was once seen searching for his body. It provided endless entertainment to his unenlightened disciples.

One even comes across people who are seriously searching for God!

TRUE SPIRITUALITY

The master was asked, "What is spirituality?"

He said, "Spirituality is that which succeeds in bringing one to inner transformation."

"But if I apply the traditional methods handed down by the masters, is that not spirituality?"

"It is not spirituality if it does not perform its function for you. A blanket is no longer a blanket if it does not keep you warm."

"So spirituality does change?"

"People change and needs change. So what was spirituality once is spirituality no more. What generally goes under the name of spirituality is merely the record of past methods."

Don't cut the person to fit the coat.

THE LITTLE FISH

"Excuse me," said an ocean fish.
"You are older than I, so
can you tell me where to find
this thing they call the ocean?"

"The ocean," said the older fish, "is the thing
you are in now."

"Oh, this? But this is water. What I'm seeking
is the ocean," said the disappointed fish
as he swam away to search elsewhere.

He came to the master in sannyasi robes. And he spoke sannyasi language: "For years I have been seeking God. I have sought him everywhere that he is said to be: on mountain peaks, the vastness of the desert, the silence of the cloister, and the dwellings of the poor."

"Have you found him?" the master asked.

"No. I have not. Have you?"

What could the master say? The evening sun was sending shafts of golden light into the room. Hundreds of sparrows were twittering on a nearby banyan tree. In the distance one could hear the sound of highway traffic. A mosquito droned a warning that it was going to strike. . . . And yet this man could sit there and say he had not found God.

After a while he left, disappointed, to search elsewhere.

*

Stop searching, little fish. There isn't anything to look *for*. All you have to do is *look*.

DID YOU HEAR THAT BIRD SING?

Hindu India developed a magnificent image to describe God's relationship with creation. God "dances" creation. He is the dancer, creation is his dance. The dance is different from the dancer; yet it has no existence apart from him. You cannot take it home in a box if it pleases you. The moment the dancer stops, the dance ceases to be.

In our quest for God, we think too much, reflect too much, talk too much. Even when we look at this dance that we call creation, we are the whole time thinking, talking (to ourselves and others), reflecting, analyzing, philosophizing. Words. Noise.

Be silent and contemplate the dance. Just look: a star, a flower, a fading leaf, a bird, a stone . . . any fragment of the dance will do. Look. Listen. Smell. Touch. Taste. And, hopefully, it won't be long before you see him—the dancer himself!

*The disciple was always complaining
to his master, "You are hiding
the final secret of Zen from me." And
he would not accept the master's denials.*

One day they were walking in the hills
when they heard a bird sing.

"Did you hear that bird sing?" said
the master.

"Yes," said the disciple.

"Well, now you know that I have hidden
nothing from you."

"Yes."

If you really heard a bird sing, if you really saw a tree . . . you would know. Beyond words and concepts.

What was that you said? You have heard dozens of birds sing and seen hundreds of trees? Ah, was it the tree you saw or the label? If you look at a tree and see a tree, you have really not seen the tree. When you look at the tree and see a miracle—then, at last, you have seen! Did your heart never fill with wordless wonder when you heard a bird in song?

I CHOP WOOD!

When the Zen master attained enlightenment
he wrote the following lines to celebrate it:

"Oh wondrous marvel:
I chop wood!
I draw water from the well!"

After enlightenment nothing really changes. The tree is still a tree; people are just what they were before and so are you. You may continue to be as moody or even-tempered, as wise or foolish. The one difference is that you see things with a different eye. You are more detached from it all now. And your heart is full of wonder.

That is the essence of contemplation: the sense of wonder.

Contemplation is different from ecstasy in that ecstasy leads to withdrawal. The enlightened contemplative continues to chop wood and draw water from the well. Contemplation is different from the perception of beauty in that the perception of beauty (a painting or a sunset) produces aesthetic delight, whereas contemplation produces wonder—no matter what it observes, a sunset or a stone.

This is the prerogative of children. They are so often in a state of wonder. So they easily slip into the Kingdom.

THE BAMBOOS

Brownie, our dog, sat looking up the tree, ears cocked, tail tensely wagging. He was attending to a monkey. No thought disturbed his total concentration, no worry for tomorrow. Brownie was the nearest thing to pure contemplation that I have ever seen.

You may have experienced some of this yourself when you were totally absorbed watching a cat at play. Here is a formula for contemplation, as good as any I know: Be totally in the present.

Drop every thought of the future, drop every thought of the past, drop every image and abstraction, and come into the present. Contemplation will arise!

After years of training, the disciple begged his master to give him enlightenment. The master led him to a bamboo grove and said, "See that bamboo, how tall it is? See that other one there, how short it is?"

And the disciple was enlightened.

They say Buddha practiced every form of asceticism known to the India of his times, in an effort to attain enlightenment. All in vain. One day he sat under a bodhi tree and enlightenment occurred. He passed on the secret of enlightenment to his disciples in words that must seem strange to the uninitiated: "When you draw in a deep breath, oh monks, be aware that you are drawing in a deep breath. And when you draw in a shallow breath, oh monks, be aware that you are drawing in a shallow breath. And when you draw in a medium-sized breath, oh monks, be aware that you are drawing in a medium-sized breath." Awareness. Attention. Absorption.

This kind of absorption one observes in little children. They are close to the Kingdom.

CONSTANT AWARENESS

No Zen student would presume to teach
others until he had lived with his
master for at least ten years.

Tenno, having completed his ten years
of apprenticeship, acquired the rank of teacher.
One day he went to visit the master
Nan-in. It was a rainy day, so Tenno
wore wooden clogs and carried an
umbrella.

When he walked in, Nan-in greeted him
with "You left your wooden clogs
and umbrella on the porch, didn't
you? Tell me, did you place your
umbrella on the right side of the
clogs or on the left?"

Tenno was embarrassed, for he did not know
the answer. He realized he lacked
awareness. So he became Nan-in's student
and labored for another ten years
to acquire constant awareness.

The person who is ceaselessly aware: the person who is
totally present at each moment: behold the master!

HOLINESS IN THE PRESENT MOMENT

Buddha was once asked, "What makes a person holy?" He replied, "Every hour is divided into a certain number of seconds and every second into a certain number of fractions. Anyone who is able to be totally present in each fraction of a second is holy."

*The Japanese warrior was captured
by his enemies and thrown into
prison. At night he could not
sleep for he was convinced that he
would be tortured the next
morning.*

*Then the words of his master
came to his mind. "Tomorrow is not
real. The only reality is now."*

*So he came to the present—and
fell asleep.*

The person over whom the future has lost its grip. How like the birds of the air and the lilies of the field. No anxieties for tomorrow. Total presence in the now. Holiness!

THE TEMPLE BELLS

The temple was built on an island and it held a thousand bells. Bells big and small, fashioned by the finest craftsmen in the world. When the wind blew or a storm raged, all the bells would peal out in a symphony that would send the heart of the hearer into raptures.

But over the centuries the island sank into the sea and, with it, the temple bells. An ancient legend said that the bells continued to peal out, ceaselessly, and could be heard by anyone who would listen. Inspired by this legend, a young man traveled thousands of miles, determined to hear those bells. He sat for days on the shore, facing the vanished island, and listened with all his might. But all he could hear was the sound of the sea. He made every effort to block it out. But to no avail; the sound of the sea seemed to flood the world.

He kept at his task for weeks. Each time he got disheartened he would listen to the village pundits, who spoke with unction of the mysterious legend.
Then his heart would be aflame . . . . only to become discouraged again when weeks of further effort yielded no results.

Finally he decided to give up the attempt. Perhaps he was not destined to hear the bells. Perhaps the legend was not true. It was his final day, and he went to the shore to say goodbye to the sea and the sky and the wind and the coconut trees. He lay on the sand, and for the first time, listened to the sound of the sea. Soon he was so lost in the sound that he was barely conscious of himself, so deep was the silence that the sound produced.

In the depth of that silence, he heard it! The tinkle of a tiny bell followed by another, and another and another . . . and soon every one of the thousand temple bells was pealing out in harmony, and his heart was rapt in joyous ecstasy.

Do you wish to hear the temple bells? Listen to the sound of the sea.

Do you wish to catch a glimpse of God? Look intently at creation.

THE WORD MADE FLESH

In the Gospel of Saint John we read:

> *The Word became flesh; he came to dwell*
> *among us . . . through him all things came*
> *to be; no single thing was created without*
> *him. All that came to be was alive*
> *with his life, and that life was the*
> *light of men. The light shines on in the dark,*
> *and the darkness has never quenched it.*

Look steadily at the *darkness*. It won't be long before you see the light. Gaze at things. It won't be long before you see the Word.

The Word became flesh; he came to dwell
among us. . . .

And stop those frantic efforts to change flesh back into words. Words, words, words!

THE MAN IDOL

An ancient Hindu story:

A shipwrecked merchant
drifted to the shore of Ceylon, where
Vibhishana was the King of the Monsters.
At the sight of him Vibhishana
became ecstatic with joy and said,
"Ah! He looks just like my Rama.
The same human form!" He then
had rich clothes and jewels put on
the merchant and worshiped him.

The Hindu mystic Ramakrishna says, "When I first heard this story I felt an indescribable delight. If God can be worshiped in images of clay, should he not be worshiped in people?"

SEARCHING IN THE WRONG PLACE

A neighbor found Nasruddin on hands and knees.

"What are you searching for, Mullah?"

"My key."

Both men got on their knees to search. After a while the neighbor said, "Where did you lose it?"

"At home."

"Good Lord! Then why are you searching here?"

"Because it's brighter here."

Search for God where you lost him.

THE QUESTION

*Said the monk, "All these mountains
and rivers and the earth and stars
—where do they come from?"*

*Said the master, "Where does your
question come from?"*

Search within!

LABEL MAKERS

Life is like heady wine.
Everyone reads the label on the bottle.
Hardly anyone tastes the wine.

*Buddha once held up a flower to his
disciples and asked each of them to
say something about it.*

29

One pronounced a
lecture. Another a poem.
Yet another a parable.
Each trying to outdo the
other in depth and erudition.

Label makers!

Mahakashyap
smiled and said nothing. Only he had
seen the flower.

If I could only *taste* a bird,
a flower,
a tree,
a human face!

But, alas, I have no time! My energy is spent deciphering
the label.

THE FORMULA

The mystic was back from the desert.
"Tell us," they said, "what God
is like."

But how could he ever tell them
what he had experienced in
his heart? Can God
be put into words?

He finally gave them a formula—so
inaccurate, so inadequate—in the hope
that some of them might be tempted
to experience it for themselves.

They seized upon the formula.
They made it a sacred text.
They imposed it on others as a holy belief.
They went to great pains to spread it in
foreign lands. Some even gave their
lives for it.

The mystic was sad. It might have
been better if he had said nothing.

THE EXPLORER

The explorer returned to his people,
who were eager to know about the
Amazon. But how could he ever put into
words the feelings that flooded his heart
when he saw exotic flowers
and heard the night-sounds of the forest;
when he sensed the danger of wild
beasts or paddled his canoe over
treacherous rapids?

He said, "Go and find out for yourselves."
To guide them
he drew a map of the river.
They pounced upon the map. They framed it
in their town hall. They made
copies of it for themselves. And all who had a

copy considered themselves experts on the
river, for did they not know its every turn
and bend, how broad it was
and how deep, where the rapids were
and where the falls?

It is said that Buddha obdurately refused to be drawn into talking about God.

He was probably familiar with the dangers of drawing maps for armchair explorers.

THOMAS AQUINAS STOPS WRITING

The story goes that Thomas Aquinas, one of the world's ablest theologians, suddenly stopped writing. When his secretary complained that his work was unfinished, Thomas replied, "Brother Reginald, some months ago I experienced something of the Absolute, so all I have ever written about God seems to me now to be like straw."

How could it be otherwise when the scholar becomes a seer?

> When the mystic came down from the
> mountain he was accosted by the
> atheist, who said sarcastically,
> "What did you bring us from that
> garden of delights you were in?"

> The mystic replied, "I had every
> intention of filling my skirt with
> flowers and giving them to my
> friends on my return.
> But while I was there
> I became so intoxicated with the fragrance of the garden
> that I let go of the skirt."

The Zen masters put it succinctly: "The one who knows, does not say. The one who says, does not know."

THE SMARTING DERVISH

A dervish was sitting peacefully by a river
when a passerby saw the bare back of his
neck and yielded to the temptation to
give it a resounding whack. He was full
of wonder at the sound his hand had made on
the fleshy neck, but the dervish,
smarting with pain,
got up to hit him back.

"Wait a minute," said the aggressor.
"You can hit me if you wish.
But first answer this question:
Was the sound of
the whack produced by my hand or by the
back of your neck?"

Said the dervish, "Answer that yourself.
My pain won't allow me to theorize. You
can afford to do so, because you don't feel
what I feel."

When the divine is experienced, one's propensity to theorize is considerably reduced.

ONE NOTE OF WISDOM

No one knows what became of Kakua after
he left the emperor's presence.
Here is the story:

Kakua was the first Japanese to study Zen
in China. He did not travel at all. He just
meditated assiduously. Whenever people found
him out and asked him to preach, he would
say a few words and escape to another part
of the forest where he would not
be disturbed.

On his return to Japan, the emperor
heard of him and commanded him to preach
at court. Kakua stood silent and helpless.
Then he pulled out a flute from
the folds of his robe, played one short
note on it, bowed profoundly to the
emperor, and disappeared.

Confucius says, "Not teach ripe person: waste of person.
Teach not ripe person: waste of words."

WHAT ARE YOU SAYING?

The master imprints his wisdom in the heart of his disciples, not in the pages of a book. The disciple might carry this wisdom for thirty or forty years, hidden in his heart, until he meets someone ready to receive it. Such was the tradition of Zen.

> The Zen master Mu-nan sent for his disciple Shoju
> one day and said, "I am an old man now, Shoju,
> and it is you who will carry on this teaching.
> Here is a book that has been handed down for
> seven generations from master to master. I have
> myself added some notes to it that you
> will find valuable. Here, keep it with you
> as a sign that I have made you my successor."

*"You had better keep the book yourself," said
Shoju. "I received your Zen without the help of
written words and I am quite content to let it be
that way."*

*"I know, I know," said Mu-nan patiently. "Even
so, the book has served seven generations
and it may be helpful to you too. Here, keep
it with you."*

*The two happened to be talking near the fireplace.
The instant the book touched Shoju's hand
he flung it into the fire. He had no
lust for written words.*

*Mu-nan, who was never known to be angry before,
shouted, "You must be crazy! What are you doing?"*

*Shoju shouted back, "You are crazy yourself!
What are you saying?"*

The guru speaks with authority of what he himself has
experienced. He quotes no books.

THE DEVIL AND HIS FRIEND

The devil once went for a walk
with a friend. They saw a man
ahead of them stoop down and
pick up something from the ground.

"What did that man find?" asked
the friend.

"A piece of truth," said the devil.

"Doesn't that disturb you?" asked
the friend.

"No," said the devil,
"I shall let him make
a belief out of it."

A religious belief is a signpost pointing the way to truth. When you cling to the signpost you are prevented from moving toward the truth because you think you have it already.

NASRUDDIN IS DEAD

Nasruddin was in a philosophical frame of mind: "Life and death—who can say what they are?" His wife, who was busy in the kitchen, overheard him and said, "You men are all alike —quite unpractical. Anyone can tell that when a man's extremities are rigid and cold, he is dead."

Nasruddin was impressed by his wife's practical wisdom. Once when he was out in the winter snow, he felt his hands and feet go numb. "I must be dead," he thought. Then came a further thought: "What am I doing walking around if I am dead? I should be lying down like a normal corpse." Which is just what he did.

An hour later, a group of travelers, finding him by the roadside, began to argue whether he was alive or dead. Nasruddin yearned to cry out, "You fools, can't you see my extremities are cold and rigid?" But he knew better than to say that, for corpses do not talk.

The travelers finally concluded he was dead, and hoisted the corpse onto their shoulders with a view to carrying it to the cemetery for burial. They hadn't gone far when they came to a forking of the ways. A fresh dispute arose among them as to which road led to the cemetery. Nasruddin put up with this for as long as he could. Then he sat up and said, "Excuse me, gentlemen, but the road that leads to the cemetery is the one to your left. I know that corpses do not speak, but I have broken the rule this once and I assure you it will not happen again."

When reality clashes with a rigidly held belief, reality is generally the loser.

BONES TO TEST OUR FAITH

A Christian scholar who held the Bible
to be literally true
was once accosted by a scientist who
said, "According to the Bible the
earth was created some five thousand
years ago. But we have discovered bones
that point to life on earth
a million years ago."

Pat came the answer: "When
God created earth five thousand
years ago, he deliberately put those
bones in to test our faith and see
if we would believe his Word
rather than scientific evidence."

Further evidence of rigid belief leading to reality distortion.

WHY GOOD PEOPLE DIE

*The village preacher was visiting the
home of an elderly parishioner and, over
a cup of coffee, he was answering some
of the questions that Grandma was putting
him.*

*"Why does the Lord send us epidemics
every so often?" asked the old woman.*

*"Well," said the preacher, "sometimes
people become so wicked they have to be
removed and so the good Lord allows the
coming of epidemics."*

*"But," objected Grandma, "then why do so
many good people get removed with the bad*

*"The good ones are summoned for witness,
explained the preacher. "The Lord wants t
give every soul a fair trial."*

There is nothing that the rigid believer
planation for.

THE MASTER DOES NOT KNOW

The seeker approached the disciple
and asked respectfully, "What is the
meaning of human life?"

The disciple consulted the works
of his master and confidently
replied, "Human life is nothing but
the expression of God's exuberance."

When the seeker addressed the master himself
with the same question,
the master said, "I do not know."

The seeker says, "I do not know." That takes honesty. The
Master says, "I do not know." That takes a mystic's mind
that knows things through nonknowing. The disciple says,
"I know." That takes ignorance, in the form of borrowed
knowledge.

LOOK INTO HIS EYES

The commander of the occupation troops said to the mayor of the mountain village, "We know you are hiding a traitor. Unless you give him up to us, we shall harass you and your people by every means in our power."

The village was, indeed, hiding a man who seemed good and innocent and was loved by all. But what could the mayor do now that the welfare of the village was at stake? Days of discussions in the Village Council led to no conclusion. So the mayor finally took the matter up with the priest. Priest and mayor spent a whole night searching the scriptures and finally came up with a text that said, "It is better that one man die to save the nation."

So the mayor handed over the innocent man, whose screams echoed through the village as he was tortured and put to death.

Twenty years later a prophet came to that village, went right up to the mayor, and said, "How could you have done this? That man was sent by God to be the savior of this country. And you handed him over to be tortured and killed."

"But where did I go wrong?" pleaded the mayor. *"The priest and I looked at the scriptures and did what they commanded."*

"That's where you went wrong," said the prophet. *"You looked at the scriptures. You should have also looked into his eyes."*

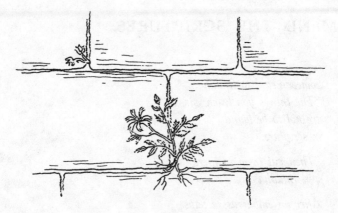

WHEAT FROM EGYPTIAN TOMBS

A handful of wheat,
five thousand years old,
was found in the tomb
of one of the kings
of ancient Egypt.
Someone planted the grains
and, to the amazement of all,
the grains came to life.

When a person is enlightened his or her words become like seeds, full of life and energy. And they can remain in seed form for centuries until they are sown in a receptive, fertile heart.

I used to think the words of scripture were dead and dry. I know now that they are full of energy and life. But it was my heart that was stony and dead, so how could anything grow there?

AMEND THE SCRIPTURES

Someone said to Buddha,
"The things you teach, sir,
are not to be found
in scripture."

"Then put them in there,"
said Buddha.

After an embarrassed pause
the man went on to say, "May I
be so bold as to suggest, sir,
that some of the things you
teach actually contradict the
scriptures?"

"Then the scriptures need amending,"
said Buddha.

*

A proposal was made at the United Nations that the scriptures of every religion be revised; everything in them that leads to intolerance or cruelty should be deleted; everything that damages the dignity of human beings should be destroyed.

When it was found that the author of the proposal was Jesus Christ, reporters rushed to his residence. His explanation was simple: "The Scripture, like the Sabbath, is for human beings," he said, "Not human beings for scripture."

THE PROFESSIONALS

My religious life has been taken over by professionals. To learn to pray I need a spiritual director; to discover God's will for me I consult an expert in discernment; to understand the Bible I consult a scripture scholar; to know if I have sinned or not I need the moral theologian; and to have my sins forgiven I kneel before the priest.

A native king in the South Sea Islands
was giving a banquet in honor of
a distinguished guest from the West.

When the time came to praise the guest, His
Majesty remained seated on the floor
while a professional orator,
engaged for the occasion,
eulogized the visitor.

After the panegyric, the guest
rose to speak.
His Majesty gently held him back.
"Don't stand up," he said. "I have engaged
an orator for you too. In our island
we don't leave public speaking to
amateurs."

I wonder, would God appreciate it if I became more amateur in my relationship with him?

THE EXPERTS

A Sufi tale:

A dead man suddenly came to life
and began to pound on the lid
of the coffin.

The lid was raised; the man
sat up. "What are you doing?" he
said to the assembled crowd.
"I am not dead."

His words were met with silent disbelief.
Finally one of the mourners said,
"Friend, both the doctors and the priests
have certified that you are dead.
So dead you are."

And he was duly buried.

THE SOUP OF THE SOUP
OF THE DUCK

A relative once came to visit Nasruddin,
bringing a duck as a gift.
So the bird was cooked and eaten.

Soon one guest after another began to
call, each claiming to be a friend of
the friend of "the man who brought you
the duck." Each one, of course, expected
to be fed and housed on the strength
of that hapless bird.

At length the mullah could stand it no
longer. One day a stranger arrived at
his house and said, "I am a friend of
the friend of the kinsman who brought
you the duck." And, like the others,
he sat down, expecting to be fed.

Nasruddin placed a bowl of steaming
water before him. "What is this?"
asked the stranger.

"This," said the mullah, "is the soup of
the soup of the duck that was brought
to me by your friend."

One hears of people who become the disciples of the disciples of the disciples of someone who had experienced the Divine.

How can you kiss through a messenger?

THE MONSTER IN THE RIVER

The village priest was distracted in
his prayers by children playing outside
his window. To get rid of them
he shouted, "There's a terrible monster
down at the river. Hurry there
and you will see him breathing fire
through his nostrils."

Soon the whole village had
heard of this monstrous apparition
and was rushing to the river.
When the priest saw this
he joined the crowd. As he panted
his way to the river, which was four
miles away, he thought, "It is true
I invented the story. Still, you
can never tell!"

A good way to believe in the gods we have created is to
convince others of their existence.

THE POISONED ARROW

A monk once said to the Lord Buddha,
"Do the souls of the just survive death?"

Characteristically, Buddha gave him no reply.

But the monk persisted. Each day he would repeat
the question and each day he would get
silence for an answer, till he could take it
no longer. He threatened to quit
unless this crucial question
was answered, for to what purpose
was he sacrificing everything to live in
the monastery if the souls of the just
perished with their bodies?"

Then the Lord Buddha, in his compassion, spoke:
"You are like a man," he said, "who was dying from
a poisoned arrow. His relatives rushed a doctor
to his side, but the man refused to have the arrow pulled out
unless
three vital questions were first answered:
First, the man who shot him, was he a white
man or a black man? Second, was he a tall man
or a short man? And third, was he a Brahmin
or an outcaste?"

The monk stayed on!

THE BABY STOPS CRYING

He claimed that, for all practical purposes, he had become an atheist. If he really thought for himself he would not believe the things his religion taught. The existence of God created more problems than it solved; life after death was a piece of wishful thinking; the scriptures and tradition had done as much harm as good. All of these things were invented to soften the loneliness and the despair of human life.

It was best to let him be. He was going through a stage of growth and discovery.

*

The master was once asked by his disciple,
> *"What is the Buddha?"*
He replied,
> *"The mind is the Buddha."*

*Another day he was asked the same question
and he replied,*
> *"No mind. No Buddha."*

The disciple was confused:
> *"But the other day you said, 'The mind is
> the Buddha.'"*

Said the master,
> *"That was to stop the baby crying. When the*
> *baby stops crying, I say, 'No mind. No*
> *Buddha.'"*

The baby in him had stopped crying and he was now ready for the truth. So he was best left alone.

*

But when he started preaching his newfound atheism to others who weren't prepared for it, someone had to curb him: "There was a time when people adored the sun: the prescientific age. Then came the scientific age and people realized that the sun was not a god; it was not even a living thing. Finally came the mystical age and Saint Francis of Assisi would call the sun his brother and speak to it in reverential love.

"Your faith was that of a frightened child. Now that you have become fearless you have no need of it. Hopefully you will move on to become a mystic someday and you will find your faith again."

Faith is the fearless search for truth. So it is not lost when one questions one's beliefs.

THE EGG

*Nasruddin earned his living selling
eggs. Someone came to his shop one day
and said, "Guess what I have in my hand."*

"Give me a clue," said Nasruddin.

*"I shall give you several: It has
the shape of an egg, the size of an
egg. It looks like an egg, tastes
like an egg, and smells like an egg.
Inside it is yellow and white. It is
liquid before it is cooked, becomes
thick when heated. It was, moreover,
laid by a hen."*

*"Aha! I know!" said Nasruddin. "It
is some sort of cake!"*

The expert misses the obvious.
The chief priest misses the Messiah.

SHOUT TO KEEP SAFE—AND CERTAIN

A prophet once came to a city
to convert its inhabitants.
At first the people listened
to his sermons, but they
gradually drifted away till
there was not a single soul
to hear the prophet when he
spoke.

One day a traveler said to him,
"Why do you go on preaching?"

Said the prophet, "In the beginning
I hoped to change these people.
If I still shout it is only to prevent
them from changing me."

RIVER WATER FOR SALE

The master's sermon that day consisted
of one enigmatic sentence.

With a wry smile he said, "All
I do is sit by the bank of the river,
selling river water."

I was so busy buying the water that I failed to see the river.

THE MEDAL

*A mother could not get her son to
come home before sunset. So she told
him that the road to their house was
haunted by ghosts who came out after dusk.*

*By the time the boy grew up he was so afraid
of ghosts that he refused to run errands at night.
So she gave him a medal and taught him that it
would protect him.*

Bad religion gives him faith in the medal.
Good religion gets him to see that ghosts do not exist.

NASRUDDIN IN CHINA

Mullah Nasruddin went to China. There
he gathered a group of disciples whom
he was preparing for enlightenment.
As soon as they became enlightened,
the disciples stopped attending
his lectures!

It is no credit to your guru that you sit at his feet forever.

THE GURU'S CAT

When the guru sat down to worship
each evening the ashram cat would
get in the way and distract the
worshipers. So he ordered that
the cat be tied during evening
worship.

After the guru died the cat
continued to be tied during evening
worship. And when the cat
expired, another cat was
brought to the ashram so that it
could be duly tied during evening
worship.

Centuries later learned treatises
were written by the guru's scholarly disciples
on the liturgical significance
of tying up a cat
while worship is performed.

LITURGICAL VESTMENTS

October 1917: The Russian Revolution is born. Human history takes a new direction.

The story goes that that very month the
Russian Church was assembled
in council. A passionate debate was in
progress about the color of the surplice to
be used in liturgical functions. Some
insisted vehemently that it had to be white.
Others, with equal vehemence,
that it had to be purple.

Coming to grips with a revolution is more of a bother than organizing a liturgy. I'd rather say my prayers than get involved in neighborhood disputes.

DANDELIONS

A man who took great pride in his lawn
found himself with a large crop of dandelions.
He tried every method he knew
to get rid of them. Still they plagued him.

Finally he wrote the Department of Agriculture.
He enumerated all the things he had tried
and closed his letter with the question:
"What shall I do now?"

In due course the reply came: "We suggest
you learn to love them."

I too had a lawn I prided myself on and I too was plagued
with dandelions that I fought with every means in my
power. So learning to love them was no easy matter.

I began by talking to them each day. Cordial. Friendly. They maintained a sullen silence. They were smarting from the war I had waged against them and were suspicious of my motives.

But it wasn't long before they smiled back. And relaxed. Soon we were good friends.

My lawn, of course, was ruined. But how attractive my garden became!

*

He was becoming blind by degrees. He fought it with every means in his power. When medicine no longer served to fight it, he fought it with his emotions. It took courage to say to him, "I suggest you learn to love your blindness."

It was a struggle. He refused to have anything to do with it in the beginning. And when he eventually brought himself to speak to his blindness his words were bitter. But he kept on speaking and the words slowly changed into words of resignation and tolerance and acceptance . . . and, one day, very much to his own surprise, they became words of friendliness . . . and love. Then came the day when he was able to put his arm around his blindness and say, "I love you." That was the day I saw him smile again.

His vision, of course, was lost forever. But how attractive his face became!

DON'T CHANGE

I was a neurotic for years. I was anxious and depressed and selfish. Everyone kept telling me to change.

I resented them, and I agreed with them, and I wanted to change, but simply couldn't, no matter how hard I tried.

What hurt the most was that, like the others, my best friend kept insisting that I change. So I felt powerless and trapped.

Then, one day, he said to me, "Don't change. I love you just as you are."

Those words were music to my ears: "Don't change. Don't change. Don't change . . . I love you as you are."

I relaxed. I came alive. And suddenly I changed!

Now I know that I couldn't really change until I found someone who would love me whether I changed or not.

Is this how you love me, God?

MY FRIEND

*Malik, son of Dinar, was much upset about the profligate
behavior of a youth who lived next door to him. For a long time
he took no action, hoping that someone else would intervene. But
when the youth's behavior became intolerable Malik went to him
and insisted that he change his ways.*

*The youth calmly replied that he was a protégé of the sultan and
so nobody could prevent him from living the way he wanted.*

*Said Malik, "I shall personally complain to the sultan." Said
the youth, "That will be quite useless, because the sultan will
never change his mind about me."*

*"I shall then denounce you to Allah," said Malik. "Allah,"
said the youth, "is far too forgiving to condemn me."*

Malik went away defeated. But after a while the youth's reputation became so bad that there was a public outcry about it. Malik decided it was his duty to attempt to reprimand him. As he was walking to the youth's house, however, he heard a voice say to him, "Do not touch my friend. He is under my protection." Malik was thrown into confusion by this and, when he was in the presence of the youth, did not know what to say.

Said the young man, "What have you come for now?" Said Malik, "I came to reprimand you. But on my way here a voice told me not to touch you, for you are under his protection."

The profligate seemed stunned. "Did he call me his friend?" he asked. But by then Malik had already left his house. Years later Malik met this man in Mecca. He had been so touched by the words of the voice that he had given up his possessions and become a wandering beggar. "I have come here in search of my Friend," he said to Malik, and died.

God, the friend of a sinner! A statement as dangerous as it is effective. I tried it on myself once. I said, "God is far too forgiving to condemn me." And I suddenly heard the Good News—for the first time in my life.

THE ARAB ASPIRANT

The Arab master Jalal ud-Din Rumi would enjoy telling the following story:

> One day Mohammed was offering
> morning prayer at the mosque. Among the
> crowd of people praying with the Prophet
> was an Arab aspirant.
>
> Mohammed began to read the Koran and recited
> the verse in which Pharaoh makes the
> claim, "I am your true God." On hearing
> this the good aspirant was so filled with
> spontaneous anger that he broke the silence
> and shouted, "The boastful son of a bitch!"
>
> The Prophet said nothing, but after prayer
> was over the others began to scold the
> Arab. "Are you not ashamed of yourself?
> Your prayer is surely displeasing to God
> because not only did you interrupt the
> holy silence of prayer but you used
> filthy language in the presence of God's
> Prophet."
>
> The poor Arab trembled with fear,
> until Gabriel appeared to the Prophet
> and said, "God sends greetings to you
> and wishes you to get these people
> to stop scolding that simple Arab;
> indeed, his spontaneous profanity
> moved my heart more than the holy prayers
> of the others."

WE ARE THREE, YOU ARE THREE

When the bishop's ship stopped at a remote island for a day, he determined to use the time as profitably as possible. He strolled along the seashore and came across three fishermen mending their nets. In pidgin English they explained to him that centuries before they had been Christianized by missionaries. "We, Christians!" they said, proudly pointing to one another.

The bishop was impressed. Did they know the Lord's Prayer? They had never heard of it. The bishop was shocked.

"What do you say, then, when you pray?"

"We lift eyes in heaven. We pray, 'We are three, you are three, have mercy on us.' The bishop was appalled at the primitive, the downright heretical nature of their prayer. So he spent the whole day teaching them the Lord's Prayer. The fishermen were poor learners, but they gave it all they had and before the bishop sailed away next day he had the satisfaction of hearing them go through the whole formula without a fault.

Months later the bishop's ship happened to pass by those islands again and the bishop, as he paced the deck saying his evening prayers, recalled with pleasure the three men on that distant island who were now able to pray, thanks to his patient efforts. While he was lost in the thought he happened to look up and noticed a spot of light in the east.
The light kept approaching the ship and, as the bishop gazed in wonder, he saw three figures walking on the water. The captain stopped the boat and everyone leaned over the rails to see this sight.

When they were within speaking distance, the bishop recognized

*his three friends, the fishermen. "Bishop!" they exclaimed. "We
hear your boat go past island and come hurry hurry meet you."*

"What is it you want?" asked the awe-stricken bishop.

*"Bishop," they said, "we so, so sorry. We forget lovely prayer.
We say, 'Our Father in heaven, holy be your name, your
kingdom come . . .' then we forget. Please tell us prayer
again."*

*The bishop felt humbled. "Go back to your homes, my friends,"
he said, "and each time you pray, say, 'We are three, you are
three, have mercy on us!'"*

PRAYER CAN BE DANGEROUS

Here is a story that was a favorite of the Sufi master Sa'di of Shiraz:

> *A certain friend of mine was delighted that his wife was pregnant. He ardently desired a male child. He prayed to God ceaselessly and made vows with this in mind.*
>
> *It so happened that his wife did give birth to a boy. My friend rejoiced and invited the whole village to a thanksgiving party.*
>
> *Years later, on my return from Mecca, I passed through my friend's village. I was told that he was in jail.*
>
> *"Why? What has he done?" I asked.*
>
> *His neighbors said, "His son got drunk, killed a man, and ran away. So his father has been arrested and put in prison."*

To ask God persistently for what we want is laudable—and perilous.

NARADA

The Hindu sage Narada started out on a pilgrimage to the temple of the Lord Vishnu. One night he stopped at a village and was given hospitality in the hut of a childless couple. Before he set out the next morning the man said to Narada, "You are going to worship Vishnu. Ask him to give me and my wife a child."

When Narada reached the temple, he said to the Lord, "That man and his wife were very kind to me. Be merciful to them and give them a child." The Lord replied, with an air of finality. "It is not in the destiny of that man to have children." So Narada performed his devotions and went back home.

Five years later he set out on the same pilgrimage and stopped at the same village and was given hospitality once again by the same couple. This time there were two little children playing at the entrance of the hut.

"Whose children are these?" asked Narada. "Mine," said the man.

Narada was intrigued. The man went on, "Soon after you left us, five years ago, a sannyasi came to our village. We put him up for the night. The next morning, before departing, he blessed my wife and me . . . and these are the fruits of his blessing."

When Narada heard this, he could not wait to get to the temple of Vishnu again. When he got there he shouted right from the entrance of the temple, "Did you not tell me that it was not in the destiny of that man to have children? He has two!"

When the Lord heard this, he laughed aloud and said, "That must be the doing of a saint. Saints have the power to change destiny!"

As they discovered at a wedding feast when the mother of Jesus got up to work a miracle before his destiny allowed it.

DESTINY IN A TOSSED COIN

The Japanese general Nobunaga
decided to attack even though he had only
one soldier to the enemy's ten. He was
sure he would win, but his soldiers
were full of doubt.

On the way to battle they stopped at a
Shinto shrine. After praying in the shrine
Nobunaga came out and said, "I shall now
toss a coin. If it is heads, we shall
win. If tails, we shall lose. Destiny
will now reveal herself."

He tossed the coin. It was heads. The
soldiers were so eager to fight that
they wiped out the enemy.

The next day an assistant said to Nobunaga,
"No one can change Destiny."

"Quite right," said Nobunaga, showing him
a doubled coin that was heads on both sides.

Who makes Destiny?

PRAYING FOR RAIN

When neurotics come to you for help, they seldom seek to be healed, for healing is painful. What they really want is to be made comfortable in their neuroses. Or, best of all, they yearn for a miracle that will heal them painlessly.

> The old man dearly loved his after-dinner pipe. One night his wife smelled something burning and shouted, "For heaven's sake, Pa! You've set your whiskers on fire."
>
> "I know it," answered the old man angrily. "Can't you see I'm praying for rain?"

THE DISABLED FOX

A fable of the Arab mystic Sa'di:

A man walking through the forest saw a fox that had lost its legs and wondered how it lived. Then he saw a tiger come in with game in its mouth. The tiger had its fill and left the rest of the meat for the fox.

The next day God fed the fox by means of the same tiger. The man began to wonder at God's greatness and said to himself, "I too shall just rest in a corner with full trust in the Lord and he will provide me with all I need."

He did this for many days but nothing happened, and he was almost at death's door when he heard a voice say, "O you who are in the path of error, open your eyes to the truth! Follow the example of the tiger and stop imitating the disabled fox."

On the street I saw a naked child, hungry and shivering in the cold. I became angry and said to God, "Why do you permit this? Why don't you do something?"

For a while God said nothing. That night he replied, quite suddenly, "I certainly did something. I made you."

THE FOOD GOD

God decided to visit the earth, so he sent an angel to survey the situation prior to his visit.

The angel returned with his report. "Most of them lack food," he said, "and most of them lack employment."

God said, "Then I shall become incarnate in the form of food for the hungry and work for the unemployed."

THE FIVE MONKS

An urgent call came to the great Lama of the North from the Lama of the South asking for a wise and holy monk to initiate the novices in the spiritual life. To everyone's astonishment, the Great Lama sent five monks instead of one. To those who inquired he said cryptically, "We will be lucky if one of them gets to the Lama."

The group had been on the road some days when a messenger came running up to them and said, "The priest of our village has died. We need someone to take his place." The village seemed a comfortable sort of place and the priest's salary was a handsome one. One of the monks was seized with pastoral concern for the people. "I should not be a Buddhist," he said, "if I did not stay on to serve these people." So he dropped out.

Some days later they happened to stay at the palace of a king who took a fancy to one of the monks. "Stay with us," said the king, "and you shall marry my daughter. And when I die, you will succeed to the throne."

The monk was attracted to the luster of kingship, so he said, "What better way to influence the people of this kingdom than to become king? I should not be a Buddhist if I did not seize this opportunity to serve the interests of religion." So he dropped out too.

The rest of the group went on their way and one night, in a hilly region, came upon a solitary hut that was occupied by a pretty girl who offered them hospitality and thanked God for having sent the monks to her. Her parents had been murdered by mountain bandits and the girl was all alone and full of anxiety. Next morning, when it was time to leave, one of the monks said, "I shall stay with this girl. I should not be a Buddhist if I did not practice compassion."

The remaining two finally came to a Buddhist village and found, to their horror, that all the villagers had abandoned their religion and were under the sway of a Hindu theologian. One of the monks said, "I owe it to these people and to the Lord Buddha himself to stay on here and win them back to the faith."

The fifth monk eventually got to the Lama of the South.

I have always dropped out for the best of reasons: to reform the liturgy, to change Church structures, to update the study of scripture, and to make theology relevant. Religious activity is my favorite escape from God.

THE JOB

Enter first applicant.

*"You understand that this is a simple test
we are giving you before we offer you the
job you have applied for?"*
"Yes."
"Well, what is two plus two?"
"Four."

Enter second applicant.

"Are you ready for the test?"
"Yes."
"Well, what is two plus two?"
"Whatever the boss says it is."

The second applicant got the job.

Which comes first, orthodoxy or the truth?

DIOGENES

The philosopher Diogenes was eating bread
and lentils for supper. He was seen by
the philosopher Aristippus, who lived comfortably
by flattering the king.

Said Aristippus, "If you would
learn to be subservient to the king
you would not have to live on
lentils."

Said Diogenes, "Learn to live on
lentils and you will
not have to cultivate
the king."

STAND UP AND BE COUNTED

*When Khrushchev pronounced his famous
denunciation of Stalin, someone
in the Congress Hall is reported
to have said, "Where were you, Comrade
Khrushchev, when all these innocent
people were being slaughtered?"*

*Khrushchev paused, looked around the
hall, and said, "Will the man who said
that kindly stand up!"*

*Tension mounted in the hall. No one
moved.*

*Then Khrushchev said, "Well,
whoever you are, you have your answer now. I
was in exactly the same position then
as you are now."*

THE TRUTH SHOP

*I could hardly believe my eyes when I saw the name of the shop:
THE TRUTH SHOP.*

*The saleswoman was very polite: What type of truth did I wish
to purchase, partial or whole? The whole truth, of course. No
deceptions for me, no defenses, no rationalizations. I wanted my
truth plain and unadulterated. She waved me on to another side
of the store.*

*The salesman there pointed to the price tag. "The price is very
high, sir," he said. "What is it?" I asked, determined to get the
whole truth, no matter what it cost. "Your security, sir," he
answered.*

*I came away with a heavy heart.
I still need the safety
of my unquestioned beliefs.*

THE NARROW PATH

God warned the people of an earthquake
that would swallow all the waters of the
land. The waters that would take their
place would make everyone insane.

Only the prophet took God seriously. He
carried huge jugs of water to his mountain
cave so that he had enough to last him
till the day he died.

Sure enough, the earthquake came and the
waters vanished and new water filled the
streams and lakes and rivers and ponds.
A few months later the prophet came down
to see what had happened. Everyone had
indeed gone mad, and attacked him,
for they thought it was **he** *who was insane.*

So the prophet went back to his mountain
cave, glad for the water he had saved.
But as time went by he found his loneliness
unbearable. He yearned for human
company, so he went down to the plains
again. Again he was rejected by the people,
for he was so unlike them.

The prophet then succumbed. He
threw away the water he had saved, drank
the new water, and joined the people
in their insanity.

The way to truth is narrow. You always walk alone.

THE PHONY

The hall was packed, mostly with elderly women. It was some sort of new religion. One of the speakers was dressed in nothing more than a turban and a loincloth. He spoke, feelingly, of the power of mind over matter.

Everyone listened spellbound. The speaker eventually returned to his place right in front of me. His neighbor turned to him and asked in a loud whisper, "Do you really believe what you said, that the body feels nothing at all and it's all in the mind?"

The phony replied, with pious conviction, "Of course I do."

"Then," said his neighbor, "would you mind changing places with me? I'm sitting in a draft."

Why do I try to practice what I preach?

If I stuck to preaching what I practice, I'd be less of a phony.

THE DREAM CONTRACT

It was nine o'clock in the morning and
Nasruddin was fast asleep. The sun had
risen in the sky, the birds were singing
in the trees, and Nasruddin's breakfast
was getting cold. So his wife woke
him up.

He woke up in a towering rage. "Why did
you wake me up just now?" he shouted.

"The sun has risen in the sky," said his
wife, "the birds are singing in the trees,
and your breakfast is getting cold."

"Breakfast be damned," he said.
"I was about to sign a contract
worth a million grams of gold."

With that he closed his eyes
to recapture his shattered dream
and those million grams of gold.

Now Nasruddin was cheating in that contract and his business partner was a tyrant.

If, on recapturing his dream, Nasruddin gives up his cheating, he will become a saint.

If he works strenuously to free the people from the oppression of the tyrant he will become a freedom fighter.

If, in the midst of his dream, he suddenly realizes that he is dreaming, he will become awakened. Enlightened.

What kind of saint or freedom fighter are you if you are still asleep?

VERY WELL, VERY WELL

A girl in the fishing village became an unwed
mother and after several beatings finally revealed
who the father of the child was: the Zen master
living on the outskirts of the village.

The villagers trooped into the master's house,
rudely disturbed his meditation, denounced him
as a hypocrite, and told him to keep the baby.
All the master said was, "Very well. Very well."

He picked the baby up
and made arrangements
for a woman from the village to feed and clothe
and look after it at his expense.

The master's name was ruined and his disciples
all abandoned him.

When this had gone on for a year, the girl
who had borne the child could stand it no longer
and finally confessed that she had lied. The father
of the child was the boy next door.

The villagers were most contrite. They prostrated
themselves at the feet of the master to beg his pardon
and to ask for the child back. The master returned
the child. And all he said was, "Very well. Very well."

The awakened person!

SONS DEAD IN A DREAM

A fisherman and his wife had
a son after many years of marriage.
The boy was the pride and joy of
his parents. Then, one day, he turned
seriously ill. A fortune was spent
on doctors and medicines. But the boy died.

His mother was utterly grief-stricken.
There wasn't a tear in his father's
eyes.

When his wife reproached him
for his total lack of sorrow,
the fisherman said,
"Let me tell you why I do not weep.
Last night I dreamed I was a king
and the proud father of eight sons.
How happy I was! Then I woke up.
Now I am greatly puzzled: Should
I weep for those boys or for
this one?"

THE GOLDEN EAGLE

A man found an eagle's egg and put it in the nest of a backyard hen. The eaglet hatched with the brood of chicks and grew up with them.

All his life the eagle did what the backyard chickens did, thinking he was a backyard chicken. He scratched the earth for worms and insects. He clucked and cackled. And he would thrash his wings and fly a few feet into the air.

Years passed and the eagle grew very old. One day he saw a magnificent bird far above him in the cloudless sky. It glided in graceful majesty among the powerful wind currents, with scarcely a beat of its strong golden wings.

The old eagle looked up in awe. "Who's that?" he asked.

"That's the eagle, the king of the birds," said his neighbor. "He belongs to the sky. We belong to the earth—we're chickens."

So the eagle lived and died a chicken, for that's what he thought he was.

THE DUCKLING

The Sufi saint Shams of Tabriz tells the following story about himself:

I have been considered a misfit since my
childhood. No one seemed to understand
me. My own father once said to me, "You
are not mad enough to be put in a madhouse,
and not withdrawn enough to be put in a
monastery. I don't know what to do with
you."

I replied, "A duck's egg was once put under
a hen. When the egg hatched the duckling
walked about with the mother hen until they
came to a pond. The duckling went straight
into the water. The hen stayed clucking
anxiously on land. Now, dear father,
I have walked into the ocean and find in it
my home. You can hardly blame me if you choose
to stay on the shore."

THE SALT DOLL

A salt doll journeyed for thousands
of miles over land, until it finally
came to the sea.

It was fascinated by this strange
moving mass, quite unlike anything
it had ever seen before.

"Who are you?" said the salt doll
to the sea.

The sea smilingly replied, "Come
in and see."

So the doll waded in.
The farther it walked into the
sea the more it dissolved, until
there was only very little of it
left. Before that last bit dis-
solved, the doll exclaimed in
wonder, "Now I know what I am!"

WHO AM I?

A tale from Attar of Nishapur:

*The lover knocked at the door of his beloved. "Who knocks?"
said the beloved from within. "It is I," said the lover.
"Go away. This house will not hold you and me."*

The rejected lover went away into the desert. There he meditated for months on end, pondering the words of the beloved. Finally he returned and knocked at the door again.

"Who knocks?"
"It is you."

The door was immediately opened.

THE TALKATIVE LOVER

A lover pressed his suit unsuccessfully
for many months, suffering the atrocious
pains of rejection. Finally his sweetheart
yielded. "Come to such and such a
place, at such and such an hour," she
said to him.

At that time and place the lover finally
found himself seated beside his beloved.
He then reached into his pocket and pulled
out a sheaf of love letters that he had
written to her over the past months.
They were passionate letters, expressing
the pain he felt and his burning desire
to experience the delights of love and
union. He began to read them to his
beloved. The hours passed by but still
he read on and on.

Finally the woman said, "What kind of a
fool are you? These letters are all about
me and your longing for me. Well, here I
am sitting with you at last and you are lost
in your stupid letters."

"Here I am with you," says God, "and you keep reflecting about me in your head, talking about me with your tongue, and searching for me in your books. When will you shut up and see?"

DROPPING THE "I"

> *Disciple:*   *I have come to offer you*
> *my service.*
>
> *Master:*   *If you dropped the "I,"*
> *service would automatically*
> *follow.*

You could give all your goods to feed the poor and your body to be burned and not have love at all.

Keep your goods and abandon the "I." Don't burn your body; burn the ego. Love will automatically follow.

DROP YOUR NOTHING

Disciple: *I have come to you with nothing in my hands.*

Master: *Then drop it at once!*

Disciple: *But how can I drop it? It is nothing.*

Master: *Then carry it around with you!*

Your *nothing* can be your most valued possession.

THE ZEN MASTER AND THE CHRISTIAN

A Christian once visited a Zen master
and said, "Allow me to read you
some sentences from the Sermon on
the Mount."

"I shall listen to them with pleasure,"
said the master.

The Christian read a few sentences
and looked up. The master smiled
and said, "Whoever said those words
was truly enlightened."

This pleased the Christian. He
read on. The master interrupted
and said,
"Those words come from
a savior of mankind."

The Christian was thrilled. He continued
to read to the end. The master
then said, "That sermon was
pronounced by someone who was radiant
with divinity."

The Christian's joy knew no bounds.
He left, determined to return and
persuade the master
to become a Christian.

On the way back home he found Jesus standing by the roadside. "Lord," he said enthusiastically, "I got that man to confess that you are divine!"

Jesus smiled and said, "And what good did it do you except to inflate your Christian ego?"

COMFORT FOR THE DEVIL

An ancient Christian legend:

When the Son of God was nailed to the cross and died, he went straight down to hell from the cross and set free all the sinners who were there in torment.

And the devil wept and mourned, for he thought he would get no more sinners for hell.

Then God said to him, "Do not weep, for I shall send you all those who are self-righteous in their condemnation of sinners. And hell shall be filled up once more until I return."

BETTER SLEEP THAN SLANDER

Sa'di of Shiraz tells this story about himself:

When I was a child I was a pious boy, fervent in prayer and devotion. One night I was keeping vigil with my father, the Holy Koran on my lap.

Everyone else in the room began to slumber and soon was sound asleep, so I said to my father, "None of these sleepers opens his eyes or raises his head to say his prayers. You would think that they were all dead."

My father replied, "My beloved son, I would rather you too were asleep like them than slandering."

THE MONK AND THE WOMAN

Two Buddhist monks, on their way to the monastery, found an exceedingly beautiful woman at the riverbank. Like them, she wished to cross the river, but the water was too high. So one of the monks lifted her onto his back and carried her across.

His fellow monk was thoroughly scandalized. For two hours he berated him on his negligence in keeping the rule: Had he forgotten he was a monk? How did he dare touch a woman? And worse, carry her across the river? What would people say? Had he not brought their holy religion into disrepute? And so on.

The offending monk patiently listened to the never-ending sermon. Finally he broke in with "Brother, I dropped that woman at the river. Are you still carrying her?"

The Arab mystic Abu Hassan Bushanja says, "The act of sinning is much less harmful than the desire and thought of it. It is one thing for the body to indulge in a pleasurable act for a moment, and an entirely different thing for the mind and heart to chew on it endlessly."

Each time I chew on the sins of others, I suspect the chewing gives me more pleasure than the sinning gives the sinner.

THE SPIRITUAL HEART ATTACK

Uncle Tom had a weak heart and the doctor had warned him to be very careful. So when the family learned that he had inherited a billion dollars from a deceased relative they feared to break the news to him lest the news give him a heart attack.

So they sought the services of the local pastor, who assured them he would find a way. "Tell me, Tom," said Father Murphy, "if God, in his mercy, were to send you a billion dollars, what would you do with it?"

"I'd give half of it to you for the Church, Father."

When he heard that, Father Murphy had a heart attack!

When the industrialist had a heart attack from pushing his industrial empire it was easy to show him his greed and selfishness. When the priest had a heart attack from pushing the Kingdom of God it was impossible to show him that this was greed and selfishness in another, more respectable disguise. Is it God's Kingdom you are pushing or yourself? The Kingdom needs no pushing. Your *anxiety* betrays you, does it not?

TO KNOW CHRIST

A dialogue between a recent convert and an unbelieving friend:

> *"So you have been converted to Christ?"*
> *"Yes."*
> *"Then you must know a great deal about*
> *him. Tell me: What country was he born*
> *in?"*
> *"I don't know."*
> *"What was his age when he died?"*
> *"I don't know."*
> *"How many sermons did he preach?"*
> *"I don't know."*
> *"You certainly know very little for a*
> *man who claims to be converted to Christ!"*
> *"You are right. I am ashamed at how little*
> *I know about him. But this much I do know:*
> *Three years ago I was a drunkard. I was in*
> *debt. My family was falling to pieces. My*
> *wife and children would dread my return*
> *home each evening. But now I have given*
> *up drink; we are out of debt; ours is now*
> *a happy home. All this Christ has done*
> *for me. This much I know*
> *of him!"*

To **really** know. That is, to be transformed by what one knows.

THE LOOK OF JESUS

In the Gospel According to Luke we read:

> But Peter said, "Man, I do not know
> what you are talking about." At that
> moment, while he was still speaking,
> a cock crew; and the Lord turned and
> looked straight at Peter . . . and Peter
> went outside and wept bitterly.

I had a fairly good relationship with the Lord. I would ask him for things, converse with him, praise him, thank him. . . .

But always I had this uncomfortable feeling that he wanted me to look at him. And I would not. I would talk, but look away when I sensed he was looking at me.

I was afraid. I should find an accusation there of some unrepented sin. I thought I should find a demand there; there would be something he wanted from me.

113

One day I finally summoned up courage and looked! There was no accusation. There was no demand. The eyes just said, "I love you."

And I walked out and, like Peter, I wept.

THE GOLDEN EGG

A reading from the scriptures:

> *This is what the Lord says: There was once a goose that laid a golden egg each day. And the farmer's wife, who owned the goose, delighted in the riches that those eggs brought her. She was an avaricious woman, however, and could not wait patiently from day to day for her daily egg. She decided to kill the goose and get the eggs all at once.*

Thus far the word of God!

> *An atheist heard that text from the scriptures and scoffed: You call that the word of God! A goose that lays golden eggs! It just goes to show the absurdity of your scriptures.*

> *When a religious scholar read that text, he reacted thus: The Lord clearly tells us that there was a goose that laid golden eggs. If the Lord says this, then it must be true, no matter how absurd it appears to our poor human minds.*

Now you will ask, as well you may, how an egg, while not ceasing to be an egg, can, at the same time, be golden. Different schools of religious thought attempt to explain it differently. But what is called for here is an act of faith in this mystery that baffles human understanding.

There was even a preacher who, inspired by that text, traveled through towns and villages zealously urging people to accept the fact that God had created golden eggs at some point in history.

It is better to teach people the evils of avarice than to promote belief in golden eggs.

GOOD NEWS

Here is the Good News proclaimed by our Lord Jesus Christ:

Jesus began to teach in parables.
* He said:*

The kingdom of God is like two brothers who were called by God to give up all they had and serve humanity.

The older responded to the call generously, though he had to wrench his heart from his family and the girl he loved and dreamed of marrying. He eventually went off to a distant land where he spent himself in the service of the poorest of the poor. A persecution arose in that country and he was arrested, falsely accused, tortured, and put to death.

And the Lord said to him, "Well done, good and faithful servant! You gave me a thousand talents' worth of service. I shall now give you a billion, billion talents' worth of reward. Enter into the joy of your Lord."

The younger boy's response to the call was less than generous. He decided to ignore it and go ahead and marry the girl he loved. He enjoyed a happy married life, his business prospered, and he became famous and rich. Occasionally he would give alms to the poor.

And when it was his turn to die, the Lord said to him, "Well done, good and faithful servant! You have given me ten talents' worth of service. I shall now give you a billion, billion talents' worth of reward. Enter into the joy of your Lord!"

The older boy was surprised when he heard that his brother was to get the same reward as he. And he was pleased. He said, "Lord, knowing this as I do, if I were to be born and live my life again, I would still do exactly what I did for you."

JONEYED AND THE BARBER

The holy man Joneyed went to Mecca in beggar's clothing.
There he saw a barber shaving a nobleman. When he asked the
barber to shave him, the barber immediately left the wealthy
man and shaved Joneyed. And he took no money from him. He
actually gave Joneyed some as alms.

Joneyed was so touched that he decided he would give to the
barber whatever he got in alms that day. It so happened that a
wealthy pilgrim came up to Joneyed and gave him a bag of gold
coins. Joneyed went up to the barber's shop that evening and
offered the gold to the barber.

The barber yelled at him, "What kind of a holy
man are you that you come to reward me for an act of love?"

*

A fantasy.

The devotee yells at the Lord, "What kind of a God are you that you dare to reward my devotions!"

The Lord replies with a smile, "I am Love. So how can I offer rewards?"

When you seek a recompense your gift becomes a bribe.

THE PHARISEE

When God walked into heaven and found that
everyone was there, he wasn't pleased at all.
He owed it to his justice, did he not, to
carry out his threats. So everyone was summoned
to his throne and the angel asked to read the
Ten Commandments.

The first commandment was announced. Said God,
"All who have broken this commandment will now
betake themselves to hell." And so it was done.

The same was done with each of the commandments.
By the time the angel came to read the seventh,
no one was left in heaven except a recluse—
smug and self-complacent.

God looked up and thought, "Only one person
left in heaven? That makes it very lonesome."
So he shouted out, "Come back, everyone!"

When the recluse heard that everyone was
forgiven, he yelled in rage, "This is unjust!
Why didn't you tell me this before?"

THE OLD WOMAN'S RELIGION

A very religious-minded old woman
was dissatisfied with all existing
religions, so she founded one
of her own.

One day a reporter, who genuinely
wanted to understand her point of
view, said to her, "Do you really
believe, as people say you do, that
no one will go to heaven except you
and your housemaid?"

The old woman pondered the question
and then replied, "Well, I'm not
so sure of Mary."

LOVE'S FORGETFULNESS

"Why do you keep talking about
my past mistakes?" said the husband.
"I thought you had forgiven
and forgotten."

"I have, indeed, forgiven and
forgotten," said the wife. "But I
want to make sure you don't forget
that I have forgiven and forgotten."

*

Sinner: *"Remember not my sins, O*
        Lord!"

Lord: *"What sins? You'll have to*
        prod my memory. I forgot them long
        ago."

Love keeps no record of wrongs (1 Cor. 13).

THE LOTUS

The guru wanted his disciples to wear a special garb that would show the world their consecration. He called it *giving witness*.

As I passed by the pond I saw a lotus in
full bloom and said,
"How lovely you are, my dear! And how
beautiful must be the God who created you!"

The lotus blushed. She was the lovelier
for being so unconscious of her beauty.

Farther on was another pond where I found
another lotus spreading her petals out
toward me and saying, quite brazenly,"Look
at my beauty and give glory to my Maker."

I walked away in disgust.

*

When I set out to *edify,* I seek to impress—and become a
well-intentioned Pharisee!

THE TURTLE

The Emperor of China sent ambassadors to a hermit living in the northern mountains. They were to invite him to become prime minister of the kingdom.

After many days of travel the ambassadors arrived. The hermitage was empty! But nearby in the middle of a river was a half-naked man, seated on a rock, fishing with a line. Could this be the man the emperor thought so highly of? Inquiries at the village proved it was. So they returned to the riverbank and, as respectfully as they could, attempted to attract the fisherman's attention.

The hermit waded through the river and stood before the messengers, barefoot, arms akimbo.

"What is it you want?"

"Honored sir, His Majesty the Emperor of China, having heard of your wisdom and your holiness, has sent us with these gifts. He invites you to accept the post of prime minister of the realm."

"Prime minister of the realm?"

"Yes, respected sir."

"Me?"

"Yes, respected sir."

"Is His Majesty out of his mind?" said the hermit as he roared with uncontrollable laughter, to the discomfiture of the ambassadors.

When he was able to control himself, the hermit said, "Tell me
—is it true that mounted over the main altar of the emperor's
chapel is a stuffed turtle whose shell is encrusted with sparkling
diamonds?"

"It is, venerable sir."

"And is it true that once a day the emperor and his household
gather to do homage to this diamond-decorated turtle?"

"It is, sir."

"Now take this turtle here, wagging his tail in the muck. Do
you think this little fellow would change places, with the turtle
in the palace?"

"No, he would not."

"Then go tell the emperor that neither would I. For no one can
be alive on a pedestal."

BAYAZID BREAKS THE RULE

Bayazid, the Moslem saint, would sometimes deliberately act against the outward forms and rituals of Islam.

It once happened that, on his way back from Mecca, he stopped at the Persian town of Rey. The townsfolk, who revered him, rushed to make him welcome and created a great stir in the town. Bayazid, who was tired of this adulation, waited till he reached the marketplace. There he bought a loaf of bread and began to munch it in full view of his followers.
It was a day of fasting in the month of Ramadan,
but Bayazid judged that his journey fully justified
the breaking of the religious law.

Not so his followers. They were so scandalized at his behavior that they promptly left him and went home. Bayazid contentedly remarked to a disciple, "Notice how the moment I did something contrary to their expectation, their veneration of me vanished."

The price you pay for veneration is conformity.

STREAKY PEOPLE

*A preacher put this question to a
class of children: "If all the good
people were white and all the bad people
were black, what color would you be?"*

*Little Mary Jane replied, "Reverend, I'd
be streaky!"*

So would the preacher. So would the mahatmas, popes, and saints.

*A man was looking for a good church to
attend and he happened to enter one in
which the congregation and the preacher
were reading from their prayer book.
They were saying, "We have left undone
those things which we ought to have
done, and we have done those things
which we ought not to have done."*

*The man dropped into a seat and sighed
with relief as he said to himself,
"Thank goodness, I've found my crowd
at last."*

Attempts to hide your streakiness will sometimes be successful, always dishonest.

MUSIC TO THE DEAF

I used to be stone deaf. I would
see people stand up and go through
all kinds of gyrations. They called
it dancing. It looked absurd to me
—until one day I heard the music!

I fail to understand why saints—and lovers—behave the
way they do. So I'm waiting for my heart to come alive.

RICHES

*Husband: "I'm going to
work hard, and someday we are going to
be rich."*

*Wife: "We are already rich, dear, for
we have each other. Someday maybe
we'll have money."*

THE CONTENTED FISHERMAN

*The rich industrialist from the North was
horrified to find the Southern fisherman
lying lazily beside his boat, smoking a pipe.*

*"Why aren't you out fishing?" said the
industrialist.*

*"Because I have caught enough fish for
the day," said the fisherman.*

"Why don't you catch some more?"

"What would I do with it?"

*"You could earn more money" was the reply.
"With that you could have a motor fixed
to your boat and go into deeper waters
and catch more fish.*

Then you would make enough to buy nylon
nets. These would bring you more fish and
more money. Soon you would have enough
money to own two boats . . . maybe even a
fleet of boats. Then you would be a rich
man like me."

"What would I do then?"

"Then you could really enjoy life."

"What do you think I am doing right now?"

Which would you rather have: a fortune or a capacity for enjoyment?

THE SEVEN JARS OF GOLD

A barber was passing under a haunted tree when he heard a voice say, "Would you like to have the seven jars of gold?" He looked around and saw no one. But his greed was aroused, so he shouted eagerly, "Yes, I certainly would." "Then go home at once," said the voice. "You will find them there."

The barber ran all the way home. Sure enough, there were the seven jars—all full of gold, except for one that was only half full. Now the barber could not bear the thought of having a half-filled jar. He felt a violent urge to fill it or he simply would not be happy.

So he had all the jewelry of his family melted into coins and poured them into the half-filled jar. But the jar remained as half-filled as before. This was exasperating! He saved and skimped and starved himself and his family. To no avail. No matter how much gold he put into the jar it remained half-filled.

So one day he begged the king to increase his salary. His salary was doubled. Again the fight to fill the jar was on. He even took to begging. The jar devoured every gold coin thrown into it but remained stubbornly half-filled.

The king now noticed how starved the barber looked. "What is wrong with you?" he asked. "You were so happy and contented when your salary was smaller. Now it has been doubled and you are so worn out and dejected. Can it be that you have the seven jars of gold with you?"

The barber was astonished, "Who told you this, Your Majesty?" he asked.

The king laughed. "But these are obviously the symptoms of the person to whom the ghost has given the seven jars. He once offered them to me. When I asked if this money could be spent or was merely to be hoarded he vanished without a word. That money cannot be spent. It only brings with it the compulsion to hoard. Go and give it back to the ghost this minute and you will be happy again."

A PARABLE ON MODERN LIFE

The animals met in assembly and began
to complain that humans were always
taking things away from them.

"They take my milk," said the cow.
"They take my eggs," said the hen.
"They take my flesh for bacon," said the hog.
"They hunt me for my oil," said the whale.

Finally the snail spoke. "I have something
they would certainly take away from me
if they could. Something they want
more than anything else.
I have TIME."

You have all the time in the world, if you would give it to yourself. What's stopping you?

HAFEZ HAYYIM

*In the last century, a tourist from
the States visited the famous Polish
rabbi Hafez Hayyim.*

*He was astonished to see that the
rabbi's home was only a simple room
filled with books. The only furniture
was a table and a bench.*

*"Rabbi, where is your furniture?"
asked the tourist.*

"Where is yours?" replied Hafez.

"Mine? But I'm only a visitor here."

"So am I," said the rabbi.

THE SKY AND THE CROW

A tale from the Bhagavata Purana:

> *A crow once flew into the sky*
> *with a piece of meat in its beak.*
> *Twenty crows set out in pursuit*
> *of it and attacked it viciously.*
>
> *The crow finally let the piece of*
> *meat drop. Its pursuers then*
> *left it alone and flew shrieking*
> *after the morsel.*
>
> *Said the crow, "I've lost the meat and*
> *gained this peaceful sky."*

Said a Zen monk,

"When my house burned down I got an unobstructed view of the moon at night!"

WHO CAN STEAL THE MOON!

The Zen master Ryokan lived a very
simple life in a little hut at the
foot of the mountain. One night,
when the master was away, a thief
broke into the hut only to discover
that there was nothing to steal.

Ryokan returned and caught the burglar.
"You have put yourself to much trouble
to visit me," he said.
"You must not go away empty-handed.
Please take my clothes and blanket
as a gift."

The thief, quite bewildered, took
the clothes and slunk off.

Ryokan sat down naked and watched
the moon. "Poor fellow," he thought
to himself, "I wish I could give
him the gorgeous moonlight."

THE DIAMOND

*The sannyasi had reached the
outskirts of the village and settled
down under a tree for the night
when a villager came running up
to him and said, "The stone! The
stone! Give me the precious stone!"*

"What stone?" asked the sannyasi.

*"Last night the Lord Shiva appeared
to me in a dream," said the villager,
"and told me that if I went to the
outskirts of the village at dusk
I should find a sannyasi who would
give me a precious stone that would
make me rich forever."*

*The sannyasi rummaged in his bag and
pulled out a stone. "He probably
meant this one," he said, as he handed
the stone over to the villager. "I found
it on a forest path some days ago. You
can certainly have it."*

The man gazed at the stone in wonder.
It was a diamond, probably the largest
diamond in the whole world, for it was
as large as a person's head.

He took the diamond and walked away.
All night he tossed about in bed,
unable to sleep. Next day at the
crack of dawn he woke the sannyasi
and said, "Give me the wealth that
makes it possible for you to give
this diamond away so easily."

PRAY FOR A CONTENTED MIND

The Lord Vishnu said to his devotee: "I am weary
of your constant petitions.
I have decided to grant you any
three things you ask for. After that,
I shall give you nothing more."

The devotee delightedly made his first
petition at once. He asked that his
wife should die so that he could marry
a better woman. His petition was
immediately granted.

But when friends and relatives gathered
for the funeral and began to recall all
the good qualities of his wife, the
devotee realized he had been hasty. He
now realized he had been blind to
all her virtues. Was he likely to find
another woman as good as her?

So he asked the Lord
to bring her back to life!
That left him with just one
petition. He was determined not
to make a mistake this time, for he
would have no chance to correct it.
He consulted widely. Some of his friends
advised him to ask for immortality. But
of what good was immortality, said others,
if he did not have good health? And of
what use was health if he had no money?
And of what use was money if he had no friends?

Years passed and he could not make up
his mind what to ask for: life or health
or wealth or power or love. Finally he
said to the Lord, "Please advise me on
what to ask for."

The Lord laughed when he saw the
man's predicament, and said, "Ask to
be content no matter what you get."

THE WORLD FAIR OF RELIGIONS

*My friend and I went to the fair. THE WORLD FAIR OF
RELIGIONS. Not a trade fair. But the competition was as
fierce, the propaganda loud.*

*At the Jewish stall we were given handouts that said that God
was all-compassionate and the Jews were his Chosen People. The
Jews. No other people were as chosen as they.*

*At the Moslem stall we learned that God was all-merciful and
Mohammed is his only Prophet. Salvation comes from listening
to God's Prophet.*

*At the Christian stall we discovered that God is love and there
is no salvation outside the Church. Join the Church or risk
eternal damnation.*

*On the way out I asked my friend, "What do you think of
God?" He replied, "He is bigoted, fanatical, and cruel."*

Back home, I said to God, "How do you put up with this sort of thing, Lord? Don't you see they have been giving you a bad name for centuries?"

God said, "It wasn't I who organized the fair. In fact, I'd be too ashamed to visit it."

DISCRIMINATION

I went right back to the religion fair.
This time I heard a speech of the High
Priest of the Balakri religion. The Prophet
Balakri, we were told, was the Messiah,
born in the fifth-century holy land of Mesambia.

I had another encounter with God that
night. "You're a great discriminator,
aren't you, God? Why does the fifth
century have to be the enlightened century
and why does Mesambia have to be
the holy land?
What's wrong with my century, for
instance? And what's wrong with my land?"

To which God replied, "A feast day is holy
because it shows that all the days
of the year are holy. And a sanctuary is
holy because it shows that all places are
sanctified. So the Messiah is called
the Son of God to show
that everyone is divine."

JESUS AT THE FOOTBALL MATCH

Jesus Christ said he had never been
to a football match. So we took him to one,
my friends and I. It was a ferocious
battle between the Protestant Punchers
and the Catholic Crusaders.

The Crusaders scored first. Jesus cheered
wildly and threw his hat high up in the
air. Then the Punchers scored. And Jesus
cheered wildly and threw his hat high up
in the air.

This seemed to puzzle the man behind us.
He tapped Jesus on the shoulder and
asked, "Which side are you rooting for,
my good man?"

"Me?" replied Jesus, visibly excited
by the game. "Oh, I'm not rooting
for either side. I'm just enjoying
the game."

The questioner turned to his neighbor
and sneered, "Hmm, an atheist!"

We took him up on this after the game. Was he in the habit of never taking sides? "I side with people rather than religions," said Jesus, "human beings rather than Sabbath."

RELIGIOUS HATRED

A tourist says to his guide, "You
have a right to be proud of your
town. I was especially impressed
with the number of churches in it.
Surely the people here must love
the Lord."

"Well," replied the cynical guide,
"they may love the Lord, but they
sure as hell hate each other."

Like the little girl who, when asked, "Who are pagans?",
replied, "Pagans are people who do not quarrel about religion."

OFFENSIVE AND DEFENSIVE PRAYER

The Catholic football team was
on its way to an important game.
A reporter boarded the train and
asked for the football coach.

"I understand," said the reporter,
"that you carry a chaplain to pray
for the success of the team.
Would you mind introducing me to
him?"

"That would be a pleasure," said
the coach. "Which one do you want
to meet, the offensive or the
defensive chaplain?"

IDEOLOGY

Here is a newspaper account of torture practiced in modern concentration camps.

The victim is bound to a metal chair. Electric shocks are then administered in increasing intensity, until the victim confesses.

The torturer cups his hand and slaps the victim on the ear repeatedly till the eardrum breaks.

A prisoner is strapped to a dentist's chair. Then the dentist drills till he strikes a nerve. The drilling goes on till the victim agrees to cooperate.

People are not naturally cruel. They become cruel when they are unhappy—or when they succumb to an ideology.

If religious people had always followed the instinct of their heart rather than the logic of their religion we would have been spared the sight of heretics burning at stakes, widows walking into funeral pyres, and millions of innocent people slaughtered in wars that are waged in the name of God.

Compassion has no ideology.

CHANGE THE WORLD
BY CHANGING ME

The Sufi Bayazid says this about himself:

> "I was a revolutionary when I
> was young and all my prayer to God was
> 'Lord, give me the energy to change
> the world.'

> "As I approached middle age and realized
> that half my life was gone without my
> changing a single soul, I changed my
> prayer to 'Lord, give me the grace to
> change all those who come in contact
> with me. Just my family and friends,
> and I shall be satisfied.'

> "Now that I am an old man and my days
> are numbered, my one prayer
> is, 'Lord, give me the grace to change
> myself.' If I had prayed for this right
> from the start I should not have wasted
> my life."

DOMESTICATED REBELS

He was a difficult man. He thought differently and acted differently from the rest of us. He questioned everything. Was he a rebel or a prophet or a psychopath or a hero? "Who can tell the difference?" we said. "And who cares, anyway?"

So we *socialized* him. We taught him to be *sensitive* to public opinion and to the feelings of others. We got him to conform. He was a comfortable person to live with now. Well *adjusted.* We had made him manageable and docile.

We congratulated him on having achieved self-conquest. He began to congratulate himself too. He did not see that it was **we** who had conquered him.

A big guy walked into the crowded room
and yelled, "Is there a fellow by the name
of Murphy here?" A little fellow stood up
and said, "I'm Murphy."

The big guy nearly killed him. He cracked
five of his ribs, he broke his nose, he
gave him two black eyes, he flung him in
a heap on the floor. Then he stomped out.

After he had gone we were amazed to see
the little fellow chuckling to himself.
"I certainly made a fool of that guy,"
he was saying softly to himself. "I'm
not Murphy! Ha, ha!"

A society that domesticates its rebels has gained its peace.
But it has lost its future.

THE LOST SHEEP

A parable for religious educators:

A sheep found a hole in the fence
and crept through it.
He wandered far
and lost his way back.

Then he realized that he was
being followed by a wolf. He ran
and ran, but the wolf kept chasing
him, until the shepherd came
and rescued him and carried him
lovingly back to the fold.

In spite of everyone's urgings
to the contrary, the shepherd refused
to nail up the hole in the
fence.

THE PERFECT APPLE

Nasruddin had barely finished his discourse when one of the scoffers in the crowd said to him, "Instead of spinning spiritual theories, why don't you show us something practical?"

Poor Nasruddin was nonplussed. "What kind of practical thing would you want me to show you?" he asked.

Pleased that he had mortified the mullah and was making an impression on the crowd, the scoffer said, "For instance, show us an apple from the garden of Paradise."

Nasruddin immediately picked up an apple and handed it to the man. "But this apple is bad on one side," said the man. "Surely a heavenly apple would be perfect."

"A celestial apple would, indeed, be perfect," said the mullah. "But given your present faculties, this is as near to a heavenly apple as you will ever get."

Can one expect to see a perfect apple with an imperfect eye?

Or detect goodness in others when one's own heart is selfish?

THE SLAVE GIRL

*A Moslem king fell passionately in love
with a slave girl and had her transferred
from the slave quarters to the palace. He
planned to marry her and make her his
favorite wife, but, mysteriously, the girl
fell seriously ill on the very day she
entered the palace.*

*She grew steadily worse. Every known
remedy was given her, but to no avail.
The poor girl now hovered between life
and death.*

*In despair the king made an offer of half
his kingdom to anyone who would cure her.
But who would attempt to cure an illness
that had baffled the best physicians of
the realm?*

*Finally a hakim appeared who asked to be
allowed to see the girl alone. After he
had spoken with her for an hour he appeared
before the throne of the king who anxiously
awaited his verdict.*

*"Your Majesty," said the hakim. "I do indeed
have an infallible cure for the girl. And so
sure am I of its effectiveness that, were it
not to succeed, I should willingly offer myself
to be beheaded. The medicine I propose
however, will prove to be an extremely painful
one—not for the girl, but for Your Majesty."*

*"Mention the medicine," shouted the king,
"and it shall be given her, no matter the
cost."*

*The hakim looked at the king with a compassionate
eye and said, "The girl is in love with one
of your servants. Give her permission to marry
him and she will be instantly cured."*

*Poor king! He wanted the girl too much to let
her go. He loved her too much to let her die.*

CONFUCIUS THE SAGE

Pu Shang once said to Confucius, "What
kind of a sage are you that you can say
that Yen Hui excels you in straightforwardness?
That in clarifying things
Tuan-mu Tz'u is superior to you? That
Chung Yu is more courageous than you?
And that Chuan-sun Shih is more dignified
than you?"

In his eagerness to get a reply Pu
Shang moved to the edge of the mat and
nearly fell off it. "If these things
are true," he said, "then why are these
four men your disciples?"

Confucius replied, "Stay right where
you are and I shall tell you. Yen Hui
knows how to be straightforward, but
he does not know how to be flexible.
Tuan-mu Tz'u knows how to clarify

things, but he does not know how
to give a simple Yes or No for an answer.
Chung Yu knows how to be courageous,
but he does not know how to be cautious.
Chuan-sun Shih knows how to be dignified,
but he does not know how to be
unassuming. This is why these four
men are glad to study under me."

The Moslem Jalal ud-Din Rumi says, "A hand that is always open or always closed is a crippled hand. A bird that cannot open and close its wings cannot fly."

O HAPPY FAULT!

The Jewish mystic Baal Shem had a
curious way of praying to God.
"Remember, Lord," he would say,
"you need me just as much as I
need you. If you did not exist,
whom would I pray to? If I did
not exist, who would do the praying?"

It brought me so much joy to think that if I had not sinned
God would have no occasion to be forgiving.

THE COCONUT

A monkey on a tree hurled a coconut
at the head of a Sufi.

The man picked it up, drank the
milk, ate the flesh, and made a
bowl from the shell.

Thank you for your criticism of me.

THE SINGER'S VOICE FILLS THE HALL

Overheard outside a concert hall:

"What a singer! His voice filled the hall."

*"Yes, several of us had to leave the hall
to make room for it!"*

*

Overheard in a spiritual counseling session:

*"How can I love God as the scriptures tell
us to? How can I give him my whole heart?"*

*"You must first empty your heart of all
created things."*

Misleading! Don't be afraid to fill your heart with the people and things you love, for the love of God won't occupy space in your heart any more than a singer's voice occupies space in a concert hall.

Love is not like a loaf of bread. If I give a chunk of the loaf to you I have less to offer to others. Love is like eucharistic bread: I receive the whole Christ. You receive the whole Christ too; and so does the next person, and the next.

You can love your mother with your whole heart; and your husband or wife; and each of your children. The wonder is that giving the whole of it to one person does not force you to give less to another. On the contrary, each one of them now gets more. For if you love only your friend and no one else it is a feeble heart that you offer. Your friend would stand to gain if you also gave it to others.

THANKS AND YES

What does it mean to *love* God? One does not love him the way one loves the people one sees and hears and touches, for God is not a *person* in our sense of the word. He is the Unknown. He is the wholly Other. He is above terms like *he* and *she, person* and *thing.*

When we say an audience fills the hall and a singer's voice fills the hall, we use the same word to refer to two totally distinct realities. When we say we love God with our whole heart and we love our friend with our whole heart, we also use the same words to express two totally distinct realities. The singer's voice does not really *fill* the hall. And we cannot really *love* God in the usual sense of the word.

To love God with one's whole heart means to say a whole-hearted Yes to life and all that life brings with it. To accept, without reservations, all that God has ordained for one's life. To have the attitude that Jesus had when he said, "Not my will, but yours be done." To love God with one's whole heart is to make one's own the words made famous by Dag Hammarskjöld:

> For all that has been, Thanks.
> To all that shall be, Yes.

This is the kind of thing one can give to God alone. In this he has no rivals. To understand that this is what it means to love God is to see at once that it doesn't come in the way of your loving your friends wholeheartedly, tenderly, passionately.

The singer's voice remains in undisputed possession of the hall, no matter how packed the hall is with people. Those people are no rival to it. The only rival is a person or a thing that causes you to weaken your attitude of *Yes* and *Thanks*.

SIMON PETER

A dialogue from the gospels:

> *"And you,"* said Jesus. *"Who do you say I am?"*
>
> Simon Peter answered, *"You are the Messiah,
> the Son of the living God."*
>
> Then Jesus said, *"Simon, son of Jonah, you
> are favored indeed! You did not learn that
> from mortal man; my heavenly Father revealed
> it to you."*

A dialogue from life:

Jesus:	And you, who do you say I am?
Christian:	You are the Son of the living God.
Jesus:	Right. But how unfortunate you are that you learned this from mortal man. It has not yet been revealed to you by my Father.
Christian:	True, Lord. I have been cheated. Somebody gave me the answers before your Father could speak. I marvel at your wisdom that you said nothing to Simon yourself, but waited for your Father to speak first.

THE SAMARITAN WOMAN

*The woman put down her water jar and
went off to the town. She said to the
people, "Come and see the man who has
told me everything I ever did. Could
this be the Messiah?"*

*

Christian: *Oh for a teacher like the Samaritan woman!
She gave no answers. She only asked a question.
It must have been tempting to
give the answer because she got it from you directly
when you said, "I am the Messiah. I
who am talking to you."*

*Many more became disciples because of
what they heard from his own lips. They
said to the woman, "It is no longer because
of what you said that we believe, for we
have heard him ourselves, and we know that
this is, indeed, the Savior of the world."*

*I have been content to learn about you at
second hand, Lord. From scriptures and
saints; from popes and preachers. I wish I
could say to all of them, "It is no longer
because of what you said that I believe, for I
have heard him myself."*

IGNATIUS OF LOYOLA

The sixteenth-century mystic Ignatius of Loyola said of himself that at the time of his conversion he had no one to turn to for guidance, so the Lord himself taught him the way a schoolteacher teaches a little child. He once declared that even if all the scriptures were destroyed, he would hold on to what they revealed because of what the Lord had taught him personally.

Christian: *I have, unfortunately, had a surfeit of people I could turn to for guidance. They badgered me with their persistent teachings till I could barely hear you through the din. It never occurred to me that I could get my knowledge firsthand from you, for they sometimes said to me, "We are all the teachers you will ever have; he who listens to us, listens to him."*

But I am wrong to blame them or to deplore their presence in my early life.

It is I who am to blame.
For I lacked the firmness to silence them;
the courage to find out for myself;
the patience to wait for your appointed time;
and the trust that someday,
somewhere, you would break your
silence and reveal yourself to me.

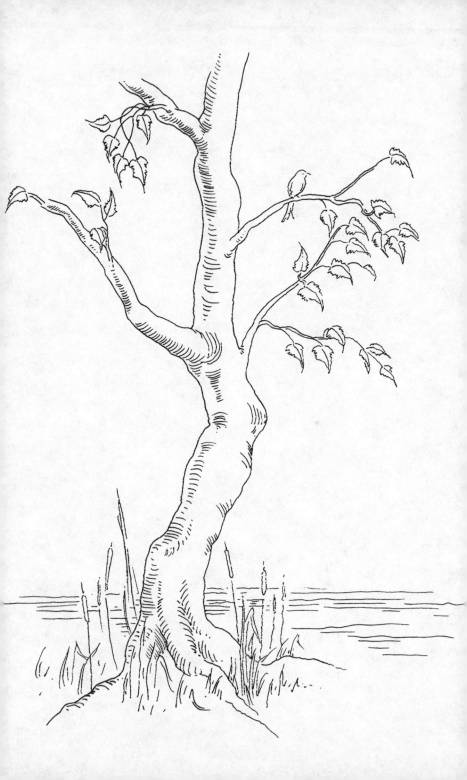